1925

The world's first sleep laboratory is opened at the University of Chicago.

1899

Italian scientist Sante de Sanctis concludes that animals dream just like people.

1950s

Scientists discover that sleep consists of cycles of different stages, repeated four or five times a night.

1912

The first electric blanket is invented by U.S. doctor Sidney I. Russell.

2013

NASA offers $18,000 for people to spend 70 days in bed with their feet up and head down, to learn how an astronaut's body might cope on a long spaceflight.

1868

German psychiatrist Wilhelm Griesinger notes that eyelids flutter during dreaming, suggesting that sleep is an active process.

1929

German Hans Berger develops the electroencephalograph (EEG) to record brain waves, and notes how brain activity changes during sleep.

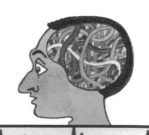

What Happens When We Sleep?

Our breathing patterns change: We breathe slowly and more regularly.

Our kidneys are less busy when we sleep, and our body produces less urine.

Our body temperature drops, reaching its lowest point during REM sleep.

Chemicals known as growth hormones are released into the bloodstream. In children, sleep is the time when the body grows. In adults, damaged cells are repaired.

Stress hormones in your body start to fall as you go to sleep, helping you to relax. But they start to rise again as you begin to wake up.

Our brains remain active while we sleep. During REM sleep, they can even become more active than when we are awake!

Our heart rate and blood pressure both go up during REM sleep.

Dreaming can occur at any point in the sleep cycle, but it tends to be most frequent during REM sleep.

Many people clench or grind their teeth while they are asleep, which is known as bruxism.

Too much "floppy" tissue in our throat or nose can make us snore. Men generally snore more than women because they have narrower air passages. As we get older these passages often get smaller, which is why old people often snore the loudest!

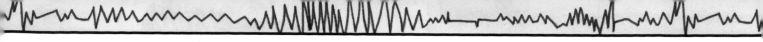

Author:

Jim Pipe studied ancient and modern history at Oxford University and spent 10 years in publishing before becoming a full-time writer. He has written numerous nonfiction books for children, many on historical subjects. He lives in Dublin, Ireland, with his wife and sons.

Artist:

Mark Bergin was born in Hastings, England, in 1961. He studied at Eastbourne College of Art and specializes in historical reconstructions, aviation, and maritime subjects. He lives in Bexhill-on-Sea with his wife and children.

Series creator:

David Salariya was born in Dundee, Scotland. He has illustrated a wide range of books and has created and designed many new series for publishers in the UK and overseas. David established The Salariya Book Company in 1989. He lives in Brighton, England, with his wife, illustrator Shirley Willis, and their son, Jonathan.

Editor: **Jacqueline Ford**

Editorial Assistant: **Mark Williams**

© The Salariya Book Company Ltd MMXVI

No part of this publication may be reproduced in whole or in part, or stored in a retrieval system, or transmitted in any form or by any means, electronic, mechanical, photocopying, recording, or otherwise, without written permission of the publisher. For information regarding permission, write to the copyright holder.

Published in Great Britain in 2016 by
The Salariya Book Company Ltd
25 Marlborough Place, Brighton BN1 1UB

ISBN-13: 978-0-531-21492-3 (lib. bdg.) 978-0-531-22442-7 (pbk.)

All rights reserved.
Published in 2016 in the United States
by Franklin Watts
An imprint of Scholastic Inc.

A CIP catalog record for this book is available
from the Library of Congress.

Printed and bound in China.
Printed on paper from sustainable sources.
1 2 3 4 5 6 7 8 9 10 R 25 24 23 22 21 20 19 18 17 16

SCHOLASTIC, FRANKLIN WATTS, and associated logos are trademarks and/or registered trademarks of Scholastic Inc.

PAPER FROM
SUSTAINABLE
FORESTS

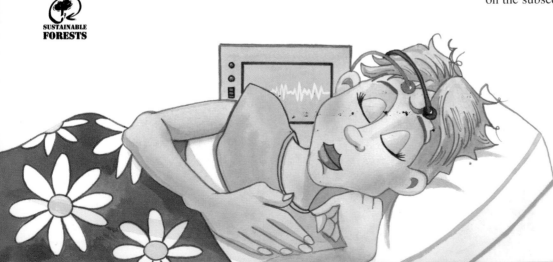

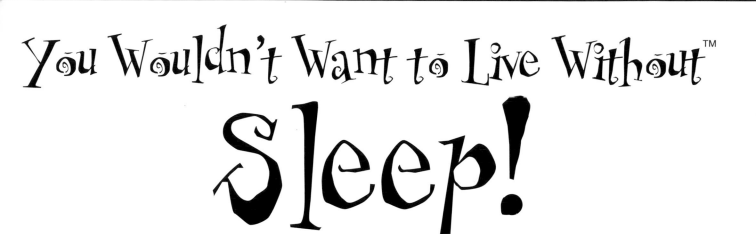

You Wouldn't Want to Live Without™
Sleep!

Written by
Jim Pipe

Illustrated by
Mark Bergin

Series created by
David Salariya

Franklin Watts®
An Imprint of Scholastic Inc.

Contents

Introduction

We all know that feeling of not being able to keep our eyes open any longer and wanting only to go to sleep. Now imagine life without a good night's sleep. It would be a one-way ticket to a tired body, a muddled head, and more often than not, grumpy behavior!

We know what sleep looks like: a person lying down or slumped in a chair with their eyes closed, breathing in a slow, steady rhythm. Most people spend a third of their life sleeping—around 25 years or more! Yet no one really knows why we do it. And how do we explain all those strange dreams about being chased or getting stuck in quicksand? What scientists do understand, however, is that sleeping soundly—and for long enough—is essential for health and happiness. Read on to learn about the benefits of sleep and why you really wouldn't want to live without it!

THANKS TO electric lighting, 24-hour services, and social media, we're living in a world where many people are not getting enough sleep. A typical adult sleeps for seven hours or less a night, but our closest relatives, such as chimps, sleep for nine or ten hours each night. Are we doing something wrong?

The Weird World of Sleep

Sleep is so familiar, and yet so incredibly odd. While our bodies rest, our hearts slow down. Meanwhile, our brains buzz with electrical and chemical activity. We never remember the moment we go to sleep.

It's hard to remember more than a small part of our dreams, and an awake person lying right next to us has no idea what we're thinking. Sleep is a mystery to scientists, too: Sometimes it can be hard to tell whether an animal is sleeping or whether it's just lying very still!

MANY ANIMALS prefer to sleep in one long session, like humans. Others like to sleep in short bursts. Either way, sleeping animals are less aware of sights, sounds, and other sensations. Heavy sleepers sleep through almost anything because their brains are better at blocking out noise, while light sleepers are woken by the slightest sound.

THE BEST WAY to check if a mammal is genuinely asleep is to monitor the pattern of electrical activity in its brain. During deep sleep, billions of individual nerve cells work in sync, generating wave after wave of tiny voltage charges. These can be detected by an electroencephalograph, or EEG, a set of electrodes placed on the scalp, first invented in 1929 by the German scientist Hans Berger.

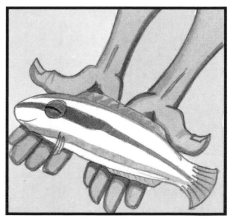

ANIMALS SLEEP in different ways, but all tend to stay still while asleep. Sloths and bats hang upside down from branches. Many birds go to sleep standing on one leg!

IN DEEP SLEEP, our muscles relax. To keep us from collapsing, our brains prevent us from sleeping unless we're lying down. Just watch someone falling asleep on a train. Their heads nod—then their brain waves wake them up!

MANY ANIMALS sleep in the same place each night. It's usually somewhere safe, like a high perch for a bird. Fish lie on the seabed or hidden in a crevice, while small mammals hide in burrows.

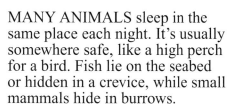

THE REEF fish *Halichoeres bivittatus* (right) is one of the world's deepest sleepers. It sleeps so soundly as it hides in the sand that it can be lifted to the surface by hand without waking up.

Do I Really Have to Sleep?

Almost all animals sleep. And with a few exceptions, such as cockroaches or migrating birds, the longer they go without sleep, the more they need it. But why do animals need to sleep at all? It makes sense to save energy when it's hard to find food, or when predators are on the prowl. Over millions of years, animal brains and bodies have evolved to gain other benefits from being asleep. For example, the chemical that makes our bodies grow is mostly released while we are asleep. That's why it's so important that children and teenagers sleep well.

THERE'S NO simple explanation for why we sleep. One theory is that the rest you get during sleep gives the cells in your body a chance to restore themselves. However, your brain is actually more active during some stages of sleep than when it is awake!

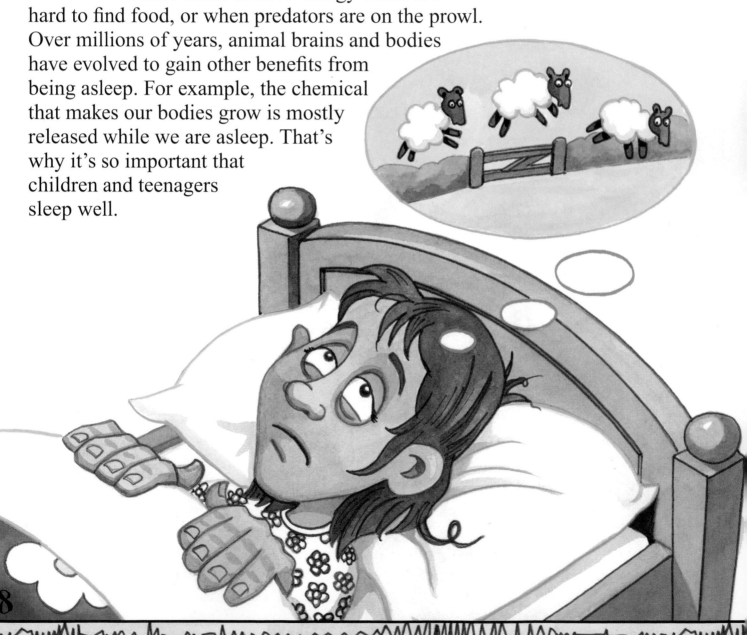

Among animals with a big brain, such as humans, sleep helps critical thinking and problem-solving. In tests, people were three times more likely to understand new ideas or tasks if they had slept well the night before learning them.

SMALL ANIMALS such as mice and shrews must eat half their body weight in food each day just to keep going. So for them, sleep is a way to save energy when they can't hunt for food.

LARGER ANIMALS such as humans or horses save only a little energy when they're asleep. That's why you might still feel tired even when you've spent all day lounging on a sofa or lying in bed!

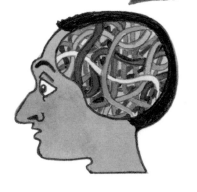

HIBERNATION IS when an animal's body shuts down during winter. It is a very deep form of sleep that allows animals such as bears and squirrels to survive the winter with little or no food. The animal's body temperature drops, and its breathing slows down.

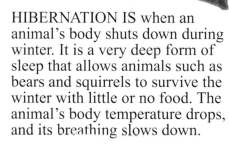

THERE IS A THEORY that while we sleep, our brain sorts through the information it learned that day, deciding what to keep and where it should go.

Back in 3 years!

SNAILS typically sleep on and off for around 14 hours, and then stay awake for the next 30 hours. Scientists believe they don't need regular sleep since there's not very much going on in their brains! Desert snails can shut down their bodies for over three years during hibernation.

Spring Summer Fall Winter

What IF I Need to Stay Awake?

Animals have developed some amazing ways to get some sleep, from switching off one side of their brain to taking lots of short naps known as microsleeps. Dolphins would drown if they fell into a deep sleep underwater, so the two halves of their brain take turns to sleep, swapping every one to three hours. Fur seals do the same when at sea, floating on the surface with one flipper paddling to keep them steady. Many birds nap with one eye closed and half the brain asleep.

TODAY, PEOPLE typically sleep through the night in one long session. In the 1400s, Italian inventor and artist Leonardo da Vinci supposedly slept for just two hours a day, taking 20-minute power naps every four hours! Astronauts, solo yacht racers, and soldiers on missions behind enemy lines have copied this sleep pattern, usually because it is too dangerous for them to be asleep for long periods.

LEONARDO inspired several other famous thinkers, including Thomas Edison and Nikola Tesla, to survive on two hours' sleep a day. In theory, sleeping like this unlocks an extra 20 years of being awake during your lifetime!

CHARLES LINDBERGH, the first solo pilot to fly nonstop across the Atlantic, greatly feared falling asleep while flying. He tried slapping his face or sniffing a bad-smelling capsule of ammonia. But nothing really worked until 24 hours into the flight, when his "body clock" told him it was a new day, and woke itself up!

Top Tip

Some companies now provide "sleep pods" to help employees nap during their lunch break. Try a midday power nap yourself, especially around 2 p.m., when your body naturally feels a little tired.

ELLEN MACARTHUR completed a record-breaking 94-day solo sailing voyage around the world in 2005. During the voyage she took 891 naps. Each lasted around 35 minutes, giving her a total of 5.5 hours of sleep per day. On several occasions she woke up just in time to avoid disaster!

THE INDUS RIVER dolphin almost never stops swimming, since it needs to be constantly alert to avoid rapidly moving objects. It sleeps for a minute at a time, having hundreds of microsleeps each day. Added up, they total about seven hours a day.

AFTERNOON POWER NAPS can help you to feel more alert and energetic afterward. In Roman times, a power nap after eating was considered a luxury: Only nobles and rich people could indulge in such a thing!

All right for some!

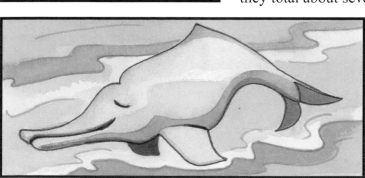

What Happens During the Night?

RAPID EYE MOVEMENT (REM). During this stage of sleep, your eyeballs move around under your eyelids. Your heart rate and breathing quicken, too, and though your brain is very active, many of your muscles may be still. During REM sleep you may also have vivid dreams.

Your body follows a 24-hour cycle of day and night, known as the circadian rhythm. You naturally start to feel drowsy when night falls. Even if it is still bright outside, a chemical in your body called melatonin makes you feel sleepy. As your body relaxes, it cools down. This is the "sleep gate," the time when your body is ready to go to sleep. Once you are asleep, your brain doesn't just turn off. It goes through several sleep stages, switching between deep non-REM sleep and REM sleep. Together, these stages form a complete sleep cycle. Each cycle usually lasts about 90 minutes and repeats four to six times during the course of the night.

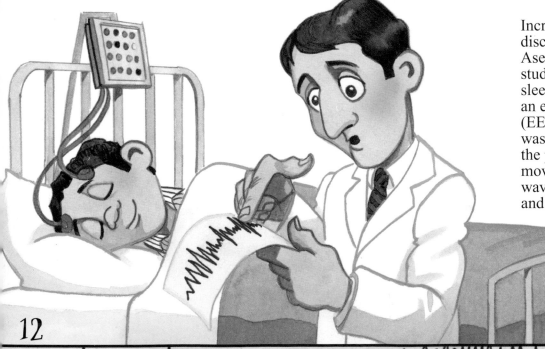

Incredibly, REM sleep was only discovered in 1952. Eugene Aserinsky, a young medical student, was monitoring the sleep of his young son with an electroencephalograph (EEG). Even though his son was fast asleep, he saw that the pens tracking his son's eye movements—and his brain waves—were swinging back and forth.

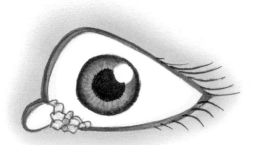

Top Tip

In a single night, you might change position 30 or 40 times—that's why you need rails on bunk beds!

THE "SLEEP" that people get in their eyes, sometimes called "eye boogers," is combined dust, blood cells, and skin cells, mixed with mucus that oozes from glands around the rim of your eyelids. The mucus helps seal your eyes when they are shut, which keeps your eyeballs moist.

The Sleep Cycle

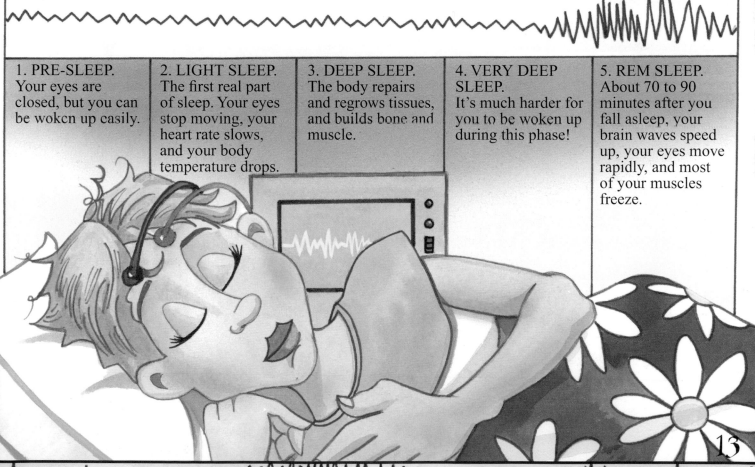

1. PRE-SLEEP. Your eyes are closed, but you can be woken up easily.

2. LIGHT SLEEP. The first real part of sleep. Your eyes stop moving, your heart rate slows, and your body temperature drops.

3. DEEP SLEEP. The body repairs and regrows tissues, and builds bone and muscle.

4. VERY DEEP SLEEP. It's much harder for you to be woken up during this phase!

5. REM SLEEP. About 70 to 90 minutes after you fall asleep, your brain waves speed up, your eyes move rapidly, and most of your muscles freeze.

Sweet Dreams?

We spend about two hours every night dreaming, with the most vivid dreams during REM sleep. Dreams are filled mostly with sights and a few sounds, but almost no smells, tastes, or touches. They can feel very real and stir up strong emotions, so that you wake up feeling afraid or annoyed with someone. While dreams and nightmares are fantasies, they often contain scenes from everyday life and people you know well. In fact, dreaming is rather like playing a virtual reality game, doing things you would never do in real life. But why our brains play these nightly shows for us remains a mystery!

Common Dreams

- Being chased or attacked
- Being trapped
- Falling or drowning
- Having problems with phones or other gadgets
- Being caught in natural or man-made disasters
- Doing badly on a test
- Being naked in public
- Losing your home
- Having car trouble
- Getting injured or sick

FOR DECADES, scientists have studied dreams, but no one knows exactly how and why we dream. One idea is that we are rehearsing what we would do in an emergency. Another is that dreams help our minds sort through everything it collects when we are awake. Some believe dreams allow your mind to replay emotions you felt during the day, such as being worried about passing a test.

Top Tip

It's said that 15 minutes after the end of a dream, we have forgotten 90 percent of its content. If you'd like to remember more, why not keep a dream diary? As soon as you wake up, write down everything you can remember.

GOING TO SLEEP isn't like turning off a light switch. As we start to nod off—or just before we wake up—we're often half-awake and half-asleep. During this time we sometimes have strange mini dreams, known as hypnagogic dreaming. The English writer Charles Dickens used these mini dreams to compose poetry.

IN A LUCID DREAM, you're aware that you're dreaming. You can change scenery, add characters, and control events. People say it feels like being inside a computer game. One way to increase the chances of having lucid dreams is to keep a dream diary. Another is sleeping, waking up, then going back to sleep again.

Going Bump in the Night

ONE WAY to stop nightmares is to avoid watching scary movies or reading scary books, especially before you go to bed. Keeping the door open or a dim light on can help, too.

If you've ever had a nightmare, you're not alone. Almost everyone gets them once in a while—adults as well as children. Nightmares are bad dreams that usually happen during REM sleep. They can make you feel scared or upset, but they're not real, and they can't harm you. Snoring, tossing and turning, groaning, or even laughing in your sleep is also common, as is grinding your teeth. But for a few unlucky people, sleep is a time for extreme behavior: sleepwalking, sleep eating, or violent actions like kicking, leaping out of bed, or slapping the person next to them.

SNORING HAPPENS when soft tissue at the back of your mouth, nose, or throat vibrates as you breathe in and out. It can be very loud and irritating. According to legend, U.S. gunslinger John Wesley Hardin killed a man snoring in the room next door by shooting through a hotel wall!

Top Tip

A good way to stop snoring is to sleep on your side or front, rather than your back, since gravity makes your tongue and other tissues sag back into your throat.

Huh?

LEE HADWIN creates bizarre artworks in his sleep, which he has no memory of drawing when he wakes up. He once covered a friend's kitchen walls in doodles!

SLEEPWALKING TEEN Rachel Ward stepped out of her bedroom window and fell 25 feet (8 meters) to the ground. Luckily, she landed feet first on the grass, and amazingly didn't break any bones!

SCOTTISH CHEF Robert Wood often gets up while asleep and heads to the kitchen to make fries and omelets. However, sleep eating can be dangerous because victims often reach for unusual or raw food, and they may burn or cut themselves as they cook.

Dead...or Just Snoozing?

TO TEST OUT his safety coffin, German inventor Adolf Gutsmuth spent several hours underground, fed by having sausages and beer delivered through a tube! Some coffins had ropes attached to bells aboveground, so the "corpse" could ring for help if he or she woke up.

In the 1700s and 1800s, large numbers of people died from diseases such as cholera and smallpox. The bodies were usually buried quickly, so doctors didn't always have time to check carefully whether the victims were really dead or had just passed out. It's no wonder that many people, including U.S. president George Washington, were terrified of being buried alive while they were asleep. So inventors came up with "safety coffins" that allowed the person inside to summon help if he or she woke up. Another nightmare of the time was waking up in the dark with the feeling that someone—or something—was sitting on your chest! This could have been caused by sleep paralysis, a rare, fleeting phenomenon where victims wake up but can't move a muscle.

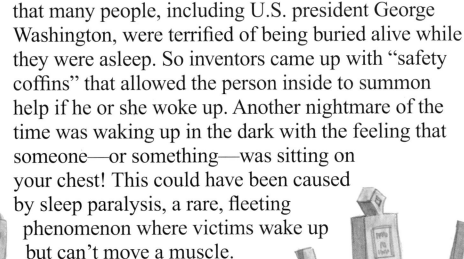

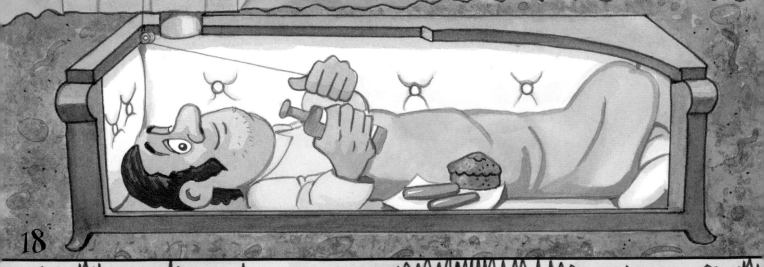

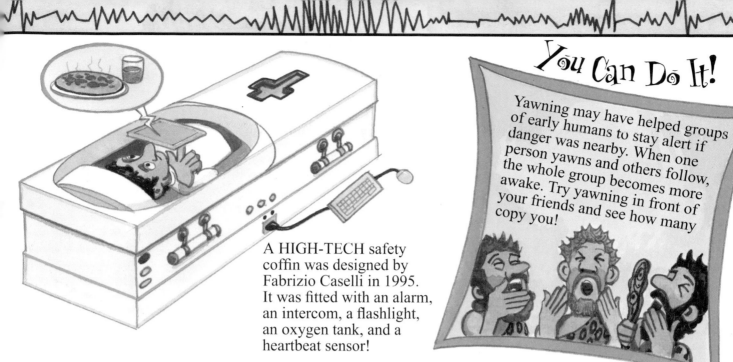

A HIGH-TECH safety coffin was designed by Fabrizio Caselli in 1995. It was fitted with an alarm, an intercom, a flashlight, an oxygen tank, and a heartbeat sensor!

You Can Do It!

Yawning may have helped groups of early humans to stay alert if danger was nearby. When one person yawns and others follow, the whole group becomes more awake. Try yawning in front of your friends and see how many copy you!

MANY ANIMALS yawn, including birds, reptiles, and even fish. It's very infectious—even just reading about it makes some people yawn! Yawning may also help to cool down our brains and help us think more clearly.

IF YOU go to sleep and wake up at the same time each night, your body learns to release a chemical about an hour before you need to wake up. That's why people often wake up five minutes before their alarm.

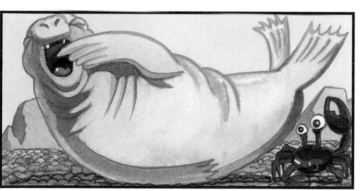

SLEEP PARALYSIS is caused by two chemicals in the brain that paralyze the victim's muscles for any amount of time from a few seconds to ten minutes. It is known as the "ghost attack" in China and "the old hag" on Newfoundland, Canada.

How Much Sleep Do I Need?

Most adults require between seven and nine hours of sleep a night. Children require different but greater amounts depending on their age (see page 28). However, we all have our own pattern of sleeping: "early birds" prefer to wake up early and go to bed early, while "night owls" go to bed late and sleep later in the morning. You may be surprised to learn that for most of history, people didn't sleep straight through the night. Before the electric lightbulb was invented by Thomas Edison in 1879, people went to bed soon after sunset. They stayed there for 10 hours or more, sleeping in two bursts of four hours, with a two- to three-hour break in the middle!

BEFORE ELECTRICITY, it was too expensive to light and heat the house all day in countries with colder winters, so families took to their beds for whole days at a time. In the 1660s, even a wealthy Londoner such as the writer Samuel Pepys stayed in bed until 11 a.m. on winter mornings.

IN A RECENT EXPERIMENT, volunteers lived in a dimly lit cave with no sense of night or day. They quickly settled down to eight hours of sleep a day, divided into two blocks with a period of quiet rest in between, just like their Stone Age ancestors.

If you wake up in the middle of the night, don't get stressed. Act like a caveman: Take it easy for a while, then go back to sleep!

I'm just not a morning person!

IF YOU WALK around like a befuddled zombie for an hour or so after waking up, you may be suffering from sleep inertia. Part of your body is still in a sleep state, so even simple tasks like putting clothing on the right way can be tricky!

SINCE ANCIENT TIMES, people have followed a seven-day week with one or two days of rest (a good time to get some extra sleep). The Romans tried an eight-day week but found it didn't work. Most cultures have had a seven-day week ever since.

Let's take the day off!

What IF I Don't Get Enough Sleep?

If you're not getting enough sleep, you may not notice—but others certainly will! Even missing out on a couple of hours' sleep can put you in a grumpy mood and make it hard to focus on anything. If you get just a few hours of sleep, you may struggle to remember information or juggle between tasks. You are more likely to pick a fight with someone, slur your speech, make risky decisions, or even experience hallucinations. You might lose long-term memories, or "remember" things that never actually happened. If you stay awake for very long periods, you'll get extremely drowsy and actually fall into microsleeps—nodding off for five to ten seconds at a time. Without any sleep at all, you would soon die.

EVEN IF you are healthy, not getting enough sleep may cause parts of your brain to shrink! Staying up all night also kills brain cells, and once the damage is done, it can't be repaired by catching up on lost sleep on the weekend.

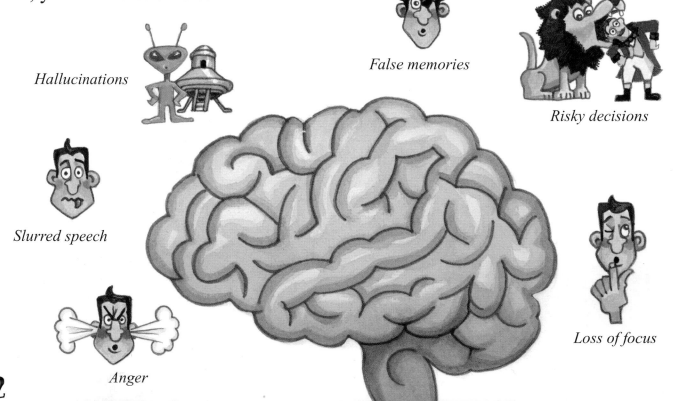

Hallucinations

False memories

Risky decisions

Slurred speech

Loss of focus

Anger

NODDING OFF is harmless in a movie theater, but a deadly mistake if you're behind the wheel of a car or working with machinery. Some 100,000 car crashes every year are caused by drivers falling asleep while driving. Many occur when the clocks are set forward and back in spring and fall, when people's body clocks are affected.

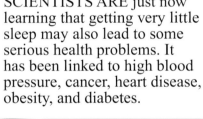

Top Tip

If you don't get enough sleep, your body releases a chemical that may give you the urge to reach for unhealthy snacks packed with salt and sugar.

TWELVE PEOPLE died in California in March 1994, when a pick-up truck crashed after the driver fell asleep.

IN FEBRUARY 2001, a sleep-deprived driver in England caused the Selby rail disaster after his car skidded onto a railway line. Ten people died, including the drivers of both trains, and 82 people were badly injured.

SCIENTISTS ARE just now learning that getting very little sleep may also lead to some serious health problems. It has been linked to high blood pressure, cancer, heart disease, obesity, and diabetes.

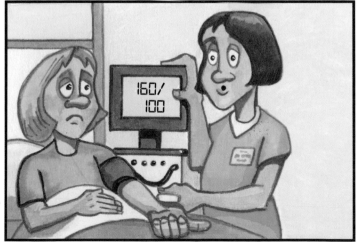

Extreme Sleep Deprivation

It's easy to tell when you haven't had enough sleep: you're sluggish, slow, and fuzzy-headed. Though your muscles can keep going even when your brain has slowed down, your body is still affected. As you can imagine, doing a difficult or dangerous job is a really bad idea when you're extremely sleepy. People are about 30 percent more likely to get injured when they work at night. Some of the world's biggest man-made disasters have also been linked to poor sleep, including the Chernobyl disaster in 1986, which happened when tired engineers made a mistake that caused a huge explosion. It was the worst nuclear power plant accident in history. Thirty-one people died and thousands more were affected by deadly radiation poisoning.

DANCE MARATHONS in the 1920s were contests to see who could dance the longest without stopping. Some competitions allowed one partner to sleep while the other kept dancing. The world record was set by a couple from Chicago who danced for 215 days!

While you are asleep, one part of your brain always stays alert—your hearing! People are more likely to wake when they hear a particular sound, such as a crying child or a barking dog.

DJ PETER TRIPP managed to stay awake for nearly eight and a half days. After three days, he began laughing hysterically. After five, he imagined seeing mice and cats scurrying around the room!

DURING THE battle of Stalingrad of World War II, Russian soldiers used loudspeakers to blare out music day and night. This caused their enemies to weaken due to lack of sleep.

A SUPER-TANKER ran aground in Alaska in 1989, spilling 11 million gallons of oil. The officer in control of the ship had slept for only six hours in two days.

KEEPING PEOPLE AWAKE is an ancient form of torture. In the 16th century, people accused of being witches were forced to stay awake for days on end. It's no surprise they ended up telling tales of flying or turning into animals!

The Future of Sleep

We now live in a world where people are just as busy at night as they are during the day, thanks to electric lighting, supermarkets that never close, and computers linking workers on different sides of the planet. In busy cities, commuter trains are full of pinched, yawning faces, and being super busy is a sign of being successful. Margaret Thatcher, a longtime prime minister of Britain, was famous for sleeping just four hours each night, while Bill Clinton slept only five or six hours a night while he was U.S. president. Will we all be expected to sleep less and less in the future?

LEGEND HAS IT that a 9th-century Ethiopian goat herder discovered coffee by accident when he noticed how excited his goats got after they nibbled on wild coffee beans. Over 1,000 years later, today's office workers often drink cups of coffee to keep themselves awake.

MORE AND MORE people are suffering from jet lag, a feeling of tiredness and confusion after a long flight. Your body finds it hard to adjust to a new time zone.

SCIENTISTS have found genes that might hold the secret to light sleeping. Imagine a new breed of super-soldiers capable of carrying out long missions without feeling drowsy or losing focus.

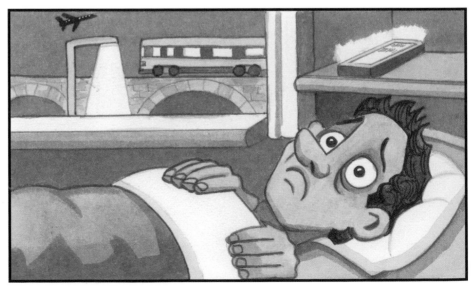

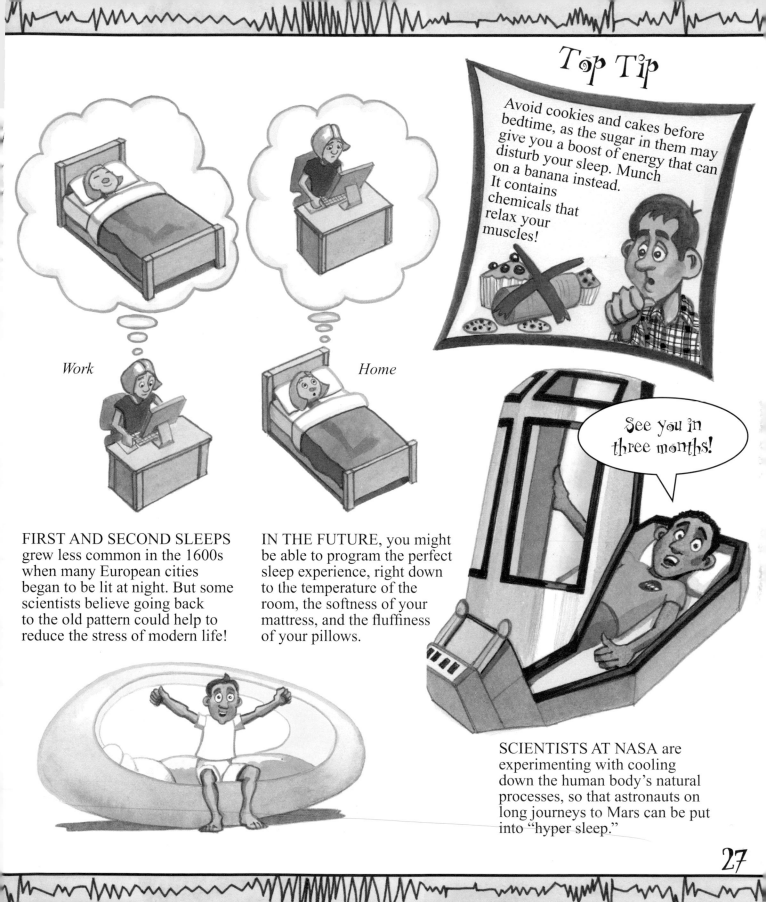

Work

Home

Top Tip

Avoid cookies and cakes before bedtime, as the sugar in them may give you a boost of energy that can disturb your sleep. Munch on a banana instead. It contains chemicals that relax your muscles!

See you in three months!

FIRST AND SECOND SLEEPS grew less common in the 1600s when many European cities began to be lit at night. But some scientists believe going back to the old pattern could help to reduce the stress of modern life!

IN THE FUTURE, you might be able to program the perfect sleep experience, right down to the temperature of the room, the softness of your mattress, and the fluffiness of your pillows.

SCIENTISTS AT NASA are experimenting with cooling down the human body's natural processes, so that astronauts on long journeys to Mars can be put into "hyper sleep."

Sleep Tight!

The amount of sleep you need changes as you age. As a newborn baby, we sleep 16 to 18 hours every day. By the age of one, we sleep for 10 to 12 hours each night and nap another 3 to 5 hours during the day. By primary school, long naps are gone, and as we grow older we sleep less, around 8 or 9 hours by the time we're 11 years old.

Most people would agree that there's nothing better than a good night's sleep. Stressful day at school? Tired after playing sports? All this can be fixed with a nice, long slumber. You awake the next day feeling calm, refreshed, and ready for anything. You wouldn't want to live without it!

DO:
- Try to go to bed and get up at the same time each day
- Get regular exercise
- Keep your bedroom quiet, dark, and cool
- Do something relaxing before going to bed

DON'T:
- Have a TV or use a computer in your bedroom
- Argue just before bed
- Go to bed too hungry or too full
- Take daytime naps longer than 20 minutes

TEENAGERS don't start producing melatonin—the sleep hormone—until 1 a.m., compared to 10 p.m. in adults. That's why it can be hard for teenagers to go to bed early. But they still need eight to nine hours of sleep—which they can't get if school starts early in the morning. That's why they need to make up for lost sleep on the weekend!

AS WE GROW OLDER, we sleep less and have less REM sleep. Elderly people wake more often in the night, and naturally turn into early birds, getting up earlier in the morning.

ALBERT EINSTEIN always slept 10 hours a night. Once, he dreamt of speeding down a mountain on a sled. When he woke up, it helped him to create his Theory of Relativity, which describes what happens when an object reaches the speed of light.

MANY FAMOUS artists and writers have been inspired by their dreams. Robert Louis Stevenson was plagued by nightmares as a child. As an adult, he used these to dream up the famous horror story of Dr. Jekyll and Mr. Hyde.

29

Glossary

Ammonia A bad-smelling substance used to wake people up.

Ancestor A person in your family who lived in the past.

Body clock The natural system in your body that controls when you need to sleep and eat.

Caffeine A natural chemical found in tea leaves and coffee beans that makes you feel more awake.

Circadian rhythm The scientific term used to describe the 24-hour cycle of waking and sleeping.

Diabetes An illness in which the body cannot control the amount of sugar in the blood.

Early bird A nickname for people who go to bed early and wake up early.

Electroencephalograph (EEG) A machine that records the electrical activity in the brain created by brain cells communicating with each other.

Glands Organs in the body that release chemicals (known as hormones) into the bloodstream. These tell the body how to work or grow, and can also help to fight disease.

Hibernation Some animals go into a very deep sleep during winter. Their bodies shut down: Breathing slows down and body temperature drops to just above freezing.

Hypnagogic dreaming A dream that happens when you are half-awake and half-asleep, often occurring first thing in the morning.

Jet lag Feeling tired or sick after a long flight crossing different time zones.

Lucid dream Any dream when you are aware that you are dreaming.

Melatonin A chemical released by the body to send it to sleep at nighttime.

Microsleep A short nap from a few seconds to several minutes.

Mucus A slimy substance produced by some parts of the body, such as your ears, nose, or throat.

NASA (National Aeronautics and Space Adminstration) The U.S. space agency, most famous for putting the first person on the moon.

Nerve cells Cells in the nervous system that carry information between the brain and the rest of the body.

Nightmare Bad or frightening dreams.

Night owl A nickname for people who go to bed late and wake up late.

Power nap A short sleep that helps to give you an energy boost.

Rapid Eye Movement (REM) Part of the sleep cycle in which the eyes move rapidly under the eyelids and dreaming often occurs.

Safety coffin A special type of coffin built in the 19th century with an alarm system in case pcople woke up after being buried alive.

Sleep deprivation When you don't get enough sleep.

Sleep paralysis When chemicals in the brain freeze, or paralyze, the victim's muscles for anything from a few seconds to several minutes.

Sleepwalking Walking, eating, and other strange behavior while asleep.

Index

Did You Know?

- The record for the longest period without sleep is 18 days, 21 hours, and 40 minutes—during a rocking-chair marathon.

- Elephants sleep standing up during non-REM sleep, but lie down for REM sleep.

- A new baby typically results in 400 to 750 hours of lost sleep for parents in the first year.

- Tiny rays of light from a digital alarm clock can be enough to disrupt your sleep cycle.

- It's impossible to tell if someone is really awake without close medical supervision. People can take catnaps with their eyes open without even being aware of it.

- French novelist Honoré de Balzac drank up to 50 cups of coffee each day, barely sleeping at all while writing his books.

- A person sleeping in a bed infested with blood-sucking bedbugs could be bitten up to 500 times a night.

- Beds can contain anywhere from 100,000 to 10 million dust mites that survive by eating your dead skin cells.

- It's said that only a national crisis would get British prime minister Winston Churchill out of bed before lunchtime!

- The world's most expensive bed is the Baldacchino Supreme Bed, costing $6.3 million. It is decorated with over 200 pounds (90 kilograms) of gold, and only two have ever been made.

Common Sleep Phrases

Sleepyhead A tired person who needs to go to sleep.

Sleep like a log To sleep heavily.

40 winks A short sleep.

Nodding off Falling asleep. If you try to sleep sitting upright, your head lowers as the neck muscles relax, then jerks up again as your brain wakes you up.

Rise and shine To wake up bright and happy.

Sleep a wink If you didn't sleep a wink, it means you didn't get any sleep at all.

Sleep like a baby To sleep very well.

Hit the hay To go to sleep. In the early 1900s, many mattresses were still stuffed with straw or hay.

Good night, sleep tight, don't let the bedbugs bite! Bedbugs are tiny insects that bite the skin of sleeping humans and animals. It's said the phrase "sleep tight" comes from the days when mattresses were supported by ropes, which needed to be pulled tight to provide a well-sprung bed.

Early to bed, early to rise, keeps a man healthy, wealthy, and wise A traditional saying.

Clinomania The scientific term for wanting to stay in bed all day.

The scratcher A common Irish expression for a bed. In the past, people would often wake up scratching after being bitten by bedbugs during the night.